Splinter of the Moon

I shall go, when God calls,
ecstatic upon silken caress
of raven night.

~ Wayne Russell
(excerpt from "When it is Time" pg. 77)

Also, by Wayne Russell

Where Angels Fear (Guarilia Genius Press 2020)

Splinter
of the Moon

Wayne Russell

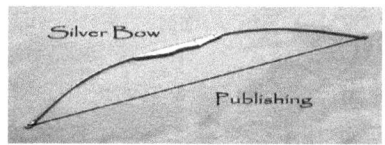

720 – Sixth Street, Box # 5
New Westminster, BC
V3C 3C5   CANADA

Title: Splinter of the Moon
Author: Wayne Russell
Publisher: Silver Bow Publishing
Cover Art: "Night of the Rose Moon" painting by Candice James
Layout/Design/Editing: Candice James

All rights reserved including the right to reproduce or translate this book or any portions thereof, in any form without the permission of the publisher. Except for the use of short passages for review purposes, no part of this book may be reproduced, in part or in whole, or transmitted in any form or by any means, either by means electronically or mechanically, including photocopying, recording, or any information or storage retrieval system without prior permission in writing from the publisher.

ISBN: 978-1-77403-284-8 paperback
ISBN: 978-1-77403-285-5 e- book

© Silver Bow Publishing 2024

Library and Archives Canada Cataloguing in Publication

Title: Splinter of the moon / Wayne Russell.
Names: Russell, Wayne (Poet), author.
Description: Poems.
Identifiers: Canadiana (print) 20240285956 | Canadiana (ebook) 20240285964 | ISBN 9781774032848
   (softcover) | ISBN 9781774032855 (Kindle)
Subjects: LCGFT: Poetry.
Classification: LCC PS3618.U772 S65 2024 | DDC 811/.6—dc23

For Jennifer

Thank you for making this journey worthwhile.

Splinter of the Moon

Table of Contents

The Birds Have Flown Away / 9
stream of thought / 10
oddity / 11
Stars / 12
Just Over the Ridge / 13
Seasonal Depression / 14
Shadows / 15
Life & Death / 16
Poetry / 17
Scotland 1991 / 18
Transgressions / 19
Here / 20
Microcosm / 21
Why I Don't Like Weekends / 22
Sunday Morning / 23
Terminus Point 2007 / 24
The Flame Always Burns / 25
On Our Way to Bedlam / 26
Red into Oblivion / 27
Start the Day Anew / 28
Life Goes On / 29
saved by zero / 30
Untitled / 31
Autumn Morning / 32
Life is Worth Living / 33
Death Echo / 34
Phenomenon / 35
Silhouette / 36
Another Day in the Life / 37
Pages / 38
Questions for Those Gone Before Us / 39
The Pendulum / 40
Hoist the Sails / 41
56 / 42
A Forest Prepares Itself for Slumber / 43
Nightmares in October / 44
When the Wolves Howl / 45
Splinter of the Moon / 46

That Poem for Her / 48
Only Love Lives On / 49
Pawns of the Sea / 50
Songs That I Sing for the Departed / 51
Don't Take My Sunshine Away / 52
Inaccessible / 53
Birds of Prey / 54
World Citizen / 55
Snow Drift / 56
Autumn Song / 57
Wolves at my Door / 58
Existentialism / 59
Indecisive / 60
That Defining Moment / 61
Sailing With the Gods of the Ocean / 62
The Vagabond / 63
When Nature Questions / 64
Room / 65
Death of a Flame Upon a Wood Fire / 66
Into the Starless Night / 67
Wilderness / 68
We Are Nothing in the Face of Eternity / 69
Sea Shanty / 70
When Nature Departs / 71
Once in a Lifetime / 72
When it is Time / 73
Our Demise / 74
Evening Raven Poem / 75
Working Hours / 76
As Time Passes / 77
Waves / 78
not of this world / 79
Dreams of You / 80
Afterglows / 81

Author Profile / 83
Afterword / 84

The Birds Have Flown Away

Birds no longer visit
the feeder hanging
from the back porch.

Squirrels have stopped
their dastardly plans
for back yard conquest.

The spoils of the feeder
now merely exist,
purposelessly;
drifting to-and-fro
in autumn breeze.

Silence fills the air.
The robins
no longer harpoon
the cool soil
seeking worms
of the earth.

Sparrows, Carolina,
Wrens, Cardinals,
Nut Hatches are now
just a distant memory.

They have all flown,
taking their songs with them,
nestled in feathers and dreams
of warmth.

stream of thought

thought comes out to play
in the depths of night;
a pen hoisted
and brought down
onto unsuspecting paper.

nocturnal creatures
rise and shine;
a toast to them
    raised.

oh natural realm,
I invite you
into this stream of thought
and onto this wilderness
of poetic capture;
a photo taken,
    yet,
with words only.

oddity

loose palace
of snow and ice
   indecent
a strangle hold
upon normalcy
you captivate me
in stealth of day
   transgress
      and
     fade
distilled with
 emotional
    night.

Stars

I cast out my net into the multitudes of stars;
they were violent and put up a tremendous struggle.

Persevering, I pulled with all my might,
simply because they were beautiful
from where I stood upon this troubled earth.

I only wanted to be whisked away
from that old nemesis of melancholy,
to toss my net into old dear goodnight, and soar.

It must have been the allure
of phosphorus shimmer;
that twinkling hypnotic sway.

It must have been that captivating beauty
of diamonds, hovering in galaxies,
millions of miles away.

What caused me to cast my old battered net,
into the thunderous cosmos?

Was it only an elusive desire to be captured,
and soar away, if only for a while?

Only to be brought back down,
with a resounding thud
of undertow and surrender,
setting feet back upon solid ground.

Just Over the Ridge

Scrapped through the ramparts,
another year breathing
its final breaths,
labored and finite.

Chiseled within
the neurotransmitters
of our minds,
photos and memories,
etched within the hippocampus,
yet locked in the vault
of the prefrontal cortex.

Are you ready to go?
Are you prepared
to solider on?

The unexpected awaits us ...
just over the ridge.

Seasonal Depression

Just when you thought
you had it all figured out,
life delivers a knockout blow.

And when you finally come back
into the realm of living,

    you find
the raven laughs
and life transformations
have taken place.

    You find out
summer has abandoned you,
and autumn's kaleidoscope vision
has taken a raincheck.

    You can see
snow is drifting aimlessly;
a catalyst to the onslaught
of painful, dead winter.

    However
you can do nothing,
but numb this pain
with antidepressants
and prayer.

    And
      you can do nothing,
but swim these frigid waters,
      just hoping for
the best possible outcome.

Shadows

Here in the shadows,
alive, but just barely,
the pain lingers on;
and away we are swept
into oblivion.

Here in the night,
captured by sounds,
adjacent to nothingness;
surrounded by emptiness.

Held to ransom by depression,
my head held tightly in her grasp,
soullessness ensuing.

Life & Death

When you leave
these corridors
of life behind.

When you leave
your dust scattered
in vacant breeze.

A trap door set.
Death is demure;
a giggle in the shadows
of heaven.

Youth will fail you.
Elder years will surprise you,
and as you turn around
the desolate corner

only one thing is certain.

Poetry

Poetry is a departure from this realm.
This life has grown as stale as
an expired loaf of bread.

Green mold spores have conquered
this over processed loaf.
My heart is hollow in my chest.

I have become numb with pills,
medication with names I can't remember,
much less pronounce; even if I try.

Poetry is a departure from this realm.
It is the breath of life;
a lifeline I cling to.

Words shaped and molded into conformity.
A departure from this life of boredom,
this life of complacency.

This soul has grown as decomposed as
a rusted out '57 Chevy.
Yet, with words scrawled out upon parchment,
it may still be worthwhile.

Scotland 1991

Standing upon boulders,
waves crashing around.
Scottish skies are dark
and ominous today.

I'm in exile
from the land of my birth,
yet in my heart
I belong to her,
land of my origin.

I feel oddly at home,
gulls crying out,
albatross perched listless
upon a dilapidated pier pole.

I am young, just 21.
I made it out alive.
My childhood is gone.
They can no longer hurt me.

I am property of the Navy now;
college upon the high seas.

A dreamer looking into
an uncertain future.

Transgressions

Nobody is perfect,
many have broken the law.
Some have left this earthly plain
and now wither away
underneath the cold earth.

Some rot away behind bars
in a prison system
overwhelmingly overpopulated.

Some are in prison
because they have taken
another person's life.

Some have robbed
banks or liquor stores.

Some have committed
    tax evasion,
or couldn't afford to pay
their child support on time.

    Nobody is perfect.
We as a species tend to become
    addicted:
some to substances,
some to alcohol,
some are hoarders,
some are embezzlers.

  And some
are bibliophiles
  just waiting
for the apocalypse.

Here

Here we are dwelling
underneath the stars,
underneath the roof
and the lights.

You're reading a book;
your intelligence arouses me
to the point where my glasses fog up.

Underneath the weight of your breath,
the pages continue turning.
You look like a cute librarian
tucked in for the night.

For us, planet earth is asleep now,
but we know wars still wage on
and people still suffer and cry.

    We know we are,
    for the most part,
      totally helpless
in the grand scheme of things.

And, yet, here we are so very comfortable
underneath the universe, the roof,
and the lights that illuminate this room
    where we dwell.

Microcosm

If you were a crow, could you stalk the night?
Would you be able to see what was going on?

This town sheds tears, just like any other.

If you were a raccoon would you huddle behind
the bars of roadside drainages, living in fear?

This town sheds blood just like any other.

If you were a deer caught in the headlights
of an oncoming automobile, would you freeze
as life slipped away?

This town sheds sweat just like any other.

Bedraggled in seedy pubs,
caught between ethereal kisses of the damned,
karaoke and alcohol can be lethal.

This town is a microcosm of a lost universe,
if you blink, you're guaranteed to miss it.

Why I Don't Like Weekends

At the end of the weekend,
weary from it all, sky gloomy
and forlorn.

Trees expired, with dead arms
outstretched and reaching.

Red brick college town,
far as anyone cares to see.
It's so cold and depressing outside;
even the young people
are hidden from view.

I'm facing the drudgery
of a work day head on,
like a deer peering into
approaching vehicle headlights.

It's raining outside, but there's a light
at the end of this dark tunnel.
I can clock out and go home now;
another weekend has expired.

Sunday Morning

The old river saunters, gray and elusive;
it winds near a smattering of trees
dotted by autumn.

Students snore in drunken oblivion,
college sanctuary,
their domain of dorm life,
independence in bloom.

I see an elderly man
wandering on the footpath,
head hung downward,
face eternal and etched into stone.

It's Sunday, and I should be in church,
but in order to get by, the bills must be paid.

To compensate,
a silent prayer is said
for the world at large;
a tear is shed within my heart
because I, too, feel empty inside.

Terminus Point October 2007

It was I who outlasted you;
it was as it should be
in this continuation of life.

Alas, all I could do was watch you
as you stumbled and plummeted
down those pathetic rickety stairs.
I watched you unraveling,
like a ball of yarn, for years;
and finally your love for booze
cost you your health.

And your heart lined with never ending despair
       cost you your sanity.
I begged you, for what seemed an eternity,
     to stop! Seek counseling!

You had so much to live for
but still you were so determined to go.
You were traveling, yet trapped,
in labyrinths of no return;
finally falling through a random portal.

It was I who witnessed
your pathetic swan dive into
the lake of fire and self-destruction.

And as your arms and legs flailed
I stood alongside the shoreline, helpless,
watching you fade from my view,
    watching you die.
Wishing there was something
I could have done to save you
     from yourself.

The Flame Always Burns

Until I burn out the night
like a flame, doused in dream,
an intriguing gaze from you.

A burning desire
in ambrosial revelation,
a forest of reckoning.

Seasonal swirl and glances given
from the cadence of life's serenade.

    Celestial maneuver,
sky's dark nurturing blanket.

We two coexisting in unison,
        always.

On Our Way to Bedlam

Did you have visions of bedlam sway?

A madness of catastrophic asylum,
the one upon the cobbles and hillside,
where no stars, no moonlight saunter,
pale and naked; as before.

Did you have visions of bedlam sway?

Were you're able to escape
   this land of visage?
Stare and judge the oceans
      from afar?

Red into Oblivion

Cascading dream,
red into oblivion.

Mountains topple,
seas drowning dry land.

The grave whistles
her name, once again.

Leaving this life is so easy,
     living is so hard.

Start The Day Anew

Early morning,
before I awoke,
the grave came to me
in a vision.

Outside the rain came down,
    soft as kittens' paws
on an obscure bedroom floor.

The alarm on my cellphone
    jolted me back
into the world of the living;
  time to go to work
    once again.

Life Goes On

Forget what you have heard.
Time does not heal all wounds.
Through the hourglass of life,
sands flow faster every day.

The house of horrors you grew up in
is still alive, haunted with the ghost
of no love and detached silence.

A Mother's bellow still reverberates,
off paint peeled walls,
with the razor sharp precision
of a surgeon's scalpel.

'You stupid child, can't you do anything right!?'

The only time his father laughed was at sitcoms,
his Bible, *'TV Guide'*; his holy water; *'Coors'*..
The echoing drunken snores and canned laughter
can still be heard if you close your eyes and listen.

So, forget what you have heard.
Time does not heal all wounds.

Through the veins of life,
blood flows colder, more labored
than ever before.

That old battle--scarred heart,
now struggles to keep up with
the rhythm of life;
but somehow it does ...
and life goes on.

saved by zero

so meekly
we tremble
beneath bombs
that descend
with wrath of gods
and powerful fists
that thrust
casting lightning bolts
of war mongers
and money to be made
by sending lambs
to the slaughter
and delicate we fade
as flowers within seasons
infused of dying embers
my art is yours too
it belongs
as your art
belongs to me
yet bloodshed
they shall keep
as their own guilty pleasures
as their own skeletons
in their own closets
built of and divided of
hearts of stone
choose wisely
what side
you are on
if any

Untitled

Angels glanced
and refused to breathe life
into that contorted night!

And into this visceral day
spat out upon white sand dunes,
        perplexities:
of a dead catastrophic universe,
dead like a malignant tumor.

I ask you this. Are we plummeting
into an abyss of our own consumer windfall?

I heard an unbeknownst glass shrine shatter
in a stealth and magnificent canyon of orange
strewn red on barren land!

Vibrant, plucked like a ripe fruit,
glistening as a dewdrop
upon a blade of grass,
on a Sunday morning.

Autumn Morning

Mornings are frigid and darkness
still consumes this patchwork quilt
of Autumn tapestry.

Deer can be seen in silhouette
grazing, the new moon sits low,
like a tigress stalking her prey.

    Leaves twirling like ballerinas,
        hypnotic in pirouette,
      dance in gentle breeze.

        Dogwoods sway.
Their branches seem to be mourning
the loss of a rejuvenating Spring hue.

Lovers are strewn casually,
down by the riverside, and basking
in earthy colored hammocks tied to trees.

The bounty of last night's drinking sprees
will be folklore; stories told with pride
like soldiers wearing shiny new medals.

Life is Worth Living

Life is precious and valuable.
It is fragile and gone
in the blink of an eye.

Everyone's life matters,
no matter what race, ethnicity,
social economic background,
or religious beliefs, or lack thereof.

Sure wish I could have
talked that kid down,
before he leapt from
the fourth story window ledge.

Sure wish I could have
called for help, for that homeless man
who died behind a lonely pub dumpster.

But I only heard people gossip about it
the next day: the kid that leapt into oblivion,
the homeless man that died outside;
cold and alone.

I often feel guilty when I'm not there
to help my fellow human being.
Especially when their mindset is
impending doom.

Life is precious and valuable.
It is fragile and gone ...
in the blink of an eye.

Death Echo

    We are ghosts
        trapped
in the purgatory of this life.

Drifting aimlessly, between
realms of heaven and hell,
translucently wandering.

Marching slowly into the
frozen undertow of death,
the ethos of ebb and flow.

Born within a whimper,
marching vulnerably,
drifting in the abstract.

    Souls picked off,
one by one, by a sniper
going by the name of
    'Grim Reaper'.

Phenomenon

In twilight, eyes closing,
an echo of ocean waves
upon sandy shorelines.

I am here safe with you,
    my love, for now,
tucked underneath sheets
    in lucid dreams.

What is this phenomenon
    of love, of life?

Cupid's bow and arrow,
pierces the forcefield
of a heart once so hardened,
yet now, molded into clay.

    Your electric touch,
the light of your blue eyes,
  lit far away galaxies;
      and now
my soul shines brightest
    thanks to you.

Phenomena can and does occur.
Miracles still happen.
God is all around us.
I realize this fully as I collapse into
blessed slumber by your side.

Silhouette

Would the raven come tomorrow
basking within its silhouette?

A tired old relic laughing upon
some heartfelt introspection?.

No specter, nor ghoul
haunted nor hunting;
for absolution.

A howl of wind written off
 as dead skulls
of the mortal damned.

And here we all stand,
 a lyric,
interested in inclination.

Sway of crass October ocean,
 frozen souls sealed,
 and lost for an eternity.

Another Day in the Life

An old man running
through the ramparts of his life.
A field of corn fading into oblivion.
Both are windswept relics.
Both are ready to die.

Out there tossed like a cork,
mad upon the raging sea,
a sailor has reached the breaking point.
In a dream, the captain ran aground.
No one aboard survived.

The straight 'A' student and a vagabond
have a chance meeting behind a dumpster.
The razor is poised within his youthful hand,
but the homeless man reaches out, just in time;
   so *'that'* life can go on
and the cycle will continue.

Pages

Finding bits of a past,
she thought was dead and gone;
yellowed paper,
gnarled by cruel hands of time.

Poetry no one will ever read,
shards of thought, scattered dreams.
Now they only collect dust.

A diary stained by time
and coffee spills.
Ghostly fingers wandering.
Smudged tears fading.

Some words,
composed in calligraphy,
gentle as the starless night.

Other words, thoughts and prayers
scrawled in grey pencil;
indecipherable.

Ink smeared, trailing off.
Pages abandoned.
Thoughts half baked,
never completely morphed
into fruition.

Questions For Those Gone Before Us

We are living our lives, one day at a time,
complacent as can be; and the river knows this.

The ravens outside our windows
know, after Autumn,
Winter shall rear his straggly snow whites
and infuse doldrum greys into the days.
The cherry blossom trees
have done their bit, for all to see.
Now they, too, lay dormant as the dead.

We are living our lives one day at a time,
nonchalant as can be; and the elderly know this.

As we age, hindsight is in great abundance.
Are we as wise as owls? I think not.

When youth has abandoned us,
like a fair-weather friend,
do we tend to think more about our legacy?

The asylum on the hill
now houses fine art and sculpture;
but if you listen long enough,
do the ghosts, roaming, whisper?

There's a cemetery out back
of the old asylum on the hill.
It cradles those that died-.

Their epitaphs have faded
beyond recognition,
along with the memory
that they ever existed.

The Pendulum

The pendulum swings, to and fro,
counting moments of days.

A candle flame flickers in a dark room,
luminous; yet knowing.

Ghosts of a disgruntled past are swirling.
Intertwined they moan.

Dusty windows are hazy
and cracked right through.

A small rodent squeaks and scampers away
into an opening in the wall.

The voices of a haunted past reverberate
within this weary room.

As seasons change,
outside this dilapidated clapboard house,
another candle has reached its expiration.

Weary arm reaching out,
the decrepit hand strikes a match.
A new candle has now been lit.
The clacking of an ancient typewriter resumes.

hoist the sails

this poison oozing
through bleak corridors
this declaration upon
uniforms in mock bravado.

i march upon these grounds
within these unknown
ancestral landscapes
oppressive past.

i can't venture into that good night
where boats with sleek design
sit composed and set to sail.

Where ravens and seagulls
     define my life
safe in the confines of childhood
and mockery is safely roped to the moors
trembling against barren landscapes
    of cloyed nothingness
   and echoing emptiness.

56

Dark cadence, and she steals the night.
This world is a cesspit of corruption and lies
that she knew and took into her early grave.

This world will chew your soul up and spit it out,
your DNA strewn upon a boiling city sidewalk.
Humanity dissipates; nothing is what it seems.

      Crushed beneath, you die.

Mother knew this, and so she drowned her woes
behind closed doors. She mourned her favorite son;
death via 22 cal; aged 26.

Mother knew this world was a cult of evil and empire.
She knew that, and quietly surrendered to the devil
and cheap ten-dollar plastic bottles of vodka worship;
dying at the age of 56.

A Forest Prepares Itself for Slumber

Moss covered trees,
relics of earth cradle,
monstrous and reaching.

Leaves strewn in silence,
upon coolness of forest floor;
a patchwork quilt.

Nature is preparing for hibernation.
Pre-Winter solace,
a healing slumber interlude.

A myriad of creatures
scuttle and scamper;
they know the time
draws near.

Nightmares in October

Derelict hours,
   haunted heart,
the time lapses
   blinding,
and life fleeting.

   Footsteps echo
behind me, trailing
  a moonlit
  nightmare
 enshrouds all.

The river knows,
yet keeps the
  secrets of
tomorrow
 tucked
safely within
 vaulted silence.

A raccoon scampers
 across an invisible
night time highway,
  never making
   it to the other
 side.

Shhhhhhhh
hisses the wheels
of the eighteen-wheeler!

This is our little secret.
One nobody ever needs
   to know about.

When the Wolves Howl

Death cadence, laughing
with a seasonal darkness,
a funeral procession,
a candle now snuffed out.

A baby crying in bassinet tilt.
Soldiers prematurely marching
towards Babylon surrender.

Ghosts remember,
educate of rambling earthy coo.
The pyre; gatherings of memories,
bones rattle in earthy cradle merger.

The echo of autumn trees sway
      and leaves fall,
love passes away in a short letter
        hastily written,
      and wolves howl ...
     as they always do.

Splinter of the Moon

Splinter of the moon,
greetings to the grandeur
of a night never reconciled.
I heard the song playing
    in a dream.

Was it in the forest roaming
of youthful endeavor?

Was it a cast iron synching,
of a river's gentle caress,
or a seagull's cry?

Was it the angry unraveling
    of a world in exile?

    Or something sung
as a mother's last lullaby?

Silver hair, and I remember
your green eyes and golden
stare; way back when.

You closed the door when you
would play that guitar song.
That song you would sing,
for your favorite son; adopted like me.

Father was too busy drinking,
his non work hours away
and Mother was too busy with
my two younger brothers:
Always in trouble. Seeking attention.
Seeking love they knew how to get.

I was the eldest the forgotten one.
Adoption wrecked my future;
birthday screwed it all.

A hole developed in a heartbeat,
wider, with each one.
The psyche engrained.
Everything took a hit.
I really was "worthless" all along.

Hello Mother? Hello Father?

Sail on splinter of the moon,
sail on into the nautical
self-loathing of a life gone by.

Another goodnight song.
Another tear upon the pillow
of childhood, played so wrong.

That Poem for Her

Had I not found you,
I shudder to think of how empty
and meaningless life would have been.

Had you not kissed me
on that aging park bench, lakeside,
in the spectacular brilliance of that day;
best day ever; at least one of them;

I often think.

Had you not whispered *yes*
not once, but twice,
to my babbling nervous proposal
in that little cabin in the woods.

I often think.

I often think what if we hadn't been married
in that little church, in that little college town,
on that perfect summer day.

I often think.

Had we not found one another, I shudder to think
of how empty and meaningless life would have been;
but we did find one another and this isn't a dream.
And I still think I'm the luckiest guy in the world;
knowing this is true ... because I am.

Only Love Lives On

The madness of the world is a driving force
peering head long into soullessness.

Youth is a mask we wear for a while,
lifting it only to reveal wrinkles of time.

Old age gallops in at breakneck speed,
but still I feel so young because
she makes me feel so young all the time.
Love is a wonderful thing.
Yet, the mirror doesn't lie; it never does.
Those neurons and molecules,
are peeling away, one layer at a time.

Collagen is nature's glue.
It gives a youthful sheen to flesh.
It keeps the wrinkles at bay,
but nothing last forever.

Youth is a mask; we wear it for a while
lifting it only to reveal slate grays,
age spots and marble graves.
   Such is life. The circle is endless.
And though this mortal coil is limited,
        love is timeless.
   No boundaries can shackle it
      nor deny it.

As the pages of Autumn softly turn,
   I hear the whispering trees,
      echoing; chanting:

        Only love lives on.
        Only love lives on.

Pawns of the Sea

Haze grey,
      the horizon,
a bow of Naval vessel smashed,
seemingly into submission.

We heard Poseidon laughing,
from the emotional depths below.

Fury of the sea, tossed all sailors aboard.
      We were just pawns
 of the government's war machine,
and a gut-wrenching bellow of nature.

We were youthful, naïve boys
trapped in the bodies of men,
held captive until enlistment time expired,
and the sea spat us out onto dry land.

Songs That I Sing for the Departed

I see the dead, complacent,
still aloof and souls set to fly.

Counter point, fizzle and betrothed.
No one remains from those days gone.

And now, once again, leaves morph
from green into the yellows and reds
and oranges of Autumn.

My ghost roaming, intertwined with nature always,
while everything prepares for hibernation yet again.

While you remain in black and white photos,
brittle and fading, epitaph etched into stone,
my ghost, too, has grown weary
and yearns for eternity.

Don't Take My Sunshine Away

A dark cloud descends;
emotional blackmail.

I am not blameless
in all of this:
a checkered past,
a brutal one.

You are not blameless.
We're both at fault;
23 years running on a quarter century,
     a cut-throat parade,
living in this untimely bantering charade.

Don't take the light away ...
don't take my sunshine.

What we have created,
let them continue on
in their own special way;
let them bask in the light
of God's golden beams.

Inaccessible

Within the hemisphere of thought,
rounding a gauntlet of time,
born forth a passage,
innocent in afterlife.

    We are thrown into
this uncharted tapestry of life.

I cannot decipher, nor figure
the organic word spewed out,
droplets upon a fading caressing night.

Living in the hierarchy
of needs, wants and desires,
held snuggly, while fires
riddle blazed night
and thought sinks,
    morbid,
in haunted day.

Bird of Prey

What was the mighty hawk,
now scattered along the roadside
of untimely demise.

    I drove past,
an unwilling witness
to the ghastly sight,
red feathers strewn
in haphazard disarray.

    The stars aligned
as I wept in solemn silence.

  Nature will win out
long after we are gone.

World Citizen

    Transfixed,
and on through the night,
bedraggled candle flame.

An equinox flair, ode to Fall,
    September;
  and there she stood ...
    late 21 or 23.

I saw her piercing eyes
through the stratosphere;
an ocean's ransom now denied.

Kaleidoscope vision, marching
as soldiers in weary souls
drawn down by morning rain
and nightmare raids.

In a society, bemused by country first,
not peering past introspective eyes
there's a world out there
with copious amounts of joy and suffering:

        All the same.
        All the time.

Snow Drift

Kindred spirits,
   snow drifts
and the owl takes refuge
     from the storm.

Field mouse appears,
from unthinkable night,
brave as a rogue shooting star.

I huddle in the safe confines
    of suburban refuge:
    regrets and bourbon,
the dark and the light intertwined.

Words spoken in homage to the dead.
      'I forgive you'
echoes the ghost of a tortured past.

Orange and red flames intermingle,
    logs are snakes hissing
    in a sputtering fire.

In a flash the power shifts
    to the owl outside,
claws snap, a stranglehold.
The mouse never stood a chance,
    and neither did the fire,
expiring right before my weary eyes.

Autumn Song

The bones of all seasons
callous unto raven night,
cricket crescendo, graveyard
dotted with memories.

    Here we are
in the throes of free fall
    underneath
Autumn gallant moon.

    Here we are,
  tattered and strewn,
leaves and souls dueling
in bleak comatose stratosphere.

    Here we are
  dancing within
 cataclysmic existence of night,
hiding from milky dawning of day.

Bark of trees
surrounding shadows,
Leaves in death posed.
Photosynthesis unexplained.

Wolves At My Door

Seasonal swirl,
time passing by
at stealth gallop.

      I hope you stay here
         between
  the yellowing pages of my life,
even when its terminus is reached.

Autumn rears his colors,
strutting around
like a multi-colored peacock
in full vibrant plumage.

Ocean waves keep rhythm
in dream-time slumber.
Winter shall appear soon.

White fang,
merciless marauders,
intruders from eternal heavens,
wolves at my door.

Existentialism

Do the bones of Nietzsche or Kierkegaard
whisper their philosophy to each other
in the onslaught of Autumn breeze?

Is all of life just a whisper?
A dream, a rebuttal or rebuke,
meaninglessness, encapsulated
within these hallowed halls
called a lifespan?

What then do we have,
if not empty days, scaling the heights
of corporate excess,
or slogging miserable
in college halls, or factories?

To scale lofty heights,
only to be returned to dust,
indentured servants of ground,
and bosom of earth.

Do the souls of those gone before,
into that good night,
now rest in peace, in paradise,
no flesh weighing them down?
No phantom feathers falling,
nor ascending as Icarus;
closer to the scalding sun.

I too shall rest for eternity
in the other worldly demise.
Existentialism personified in spirit.

Indecisive

The ravage of synthesis,
bone-pearl night,
glazed bronze stars,
phosphorus and low mass,
end of a life cycle.

A symphony of love,
unleashed into the wilderness,
graveyard in ruins, a druid palace
in mock prayer.

Wounded heart river,
hyperactive racoons,
conductors of their own
oblivious domain.

A fox crosses their way,
the world at large
completes it slide
into madness.

That Defining Moment

And here it is, languid thought,
youthful, only in my mind;
and years ago, there she stood,
alone, as did I.

I did not know of her existence,
      no ... not yet.
The seasons passed.
Along the river bed,
cherry blossoms flowed
counting loneliness in moments
as the autumn dogwoods swayed
in kaleidoscope strut.

Days morphed into years,
then solemn Winter appeared
    in white robes.

    Early March. Hark!
    Arrival of an angel
injected into the dullness of my life.
  My heart leapt for joy, at last.

    Spellbound by that first kiss,
the lake and I shall keep that moment safe.

The passersby have forgotten and moved on.
    Life is perpetual motion after all.

Sailing With the Gods of the Ocean

Where we were, gray skies
and red hearts of youth,
lost in flights of fulfillment,
we took leave of our birth land,
partaking of our roots land.

Upon the mighty beast we sailed,
    haze gray and underway,
ocean swelling until it almost burst
and devoured our wayward and mortal coil.

We were youthful creatures and so naive
following our very own *Captain Ahab*
        into the abyss
conceived of Poseidon's galloping wrath
   on a cold, heartless, metal beast.

We sailed the sunsets of oblivion into
the hellish heat and soul possessing cold,
     never questioning,
  just obeying steely commands
barked out by the gods we sailed with.

The Vagabond

Swept under the bottom rung of society,
a vagabond and wanderer.

He used to care and be continuous
to the state of a world exploding
all around him.

Yet somewhere along the way,
he lost touch with reality,
a crazy exile, lost in the night,
drifting with icy breeze.

He hops trains,
rusted and bruised in his mind,
broken by this cruel
and self-serving world.

I saw him yesterday,
behind the scorned dumpster
of consumerism's nightmare;
a tattered, unraveling ball of yarn.

He spat upon the cobbles,
and muttered obscenities
to random passersby.

I passed him a crumpled 20,
his eyes lit up, and in an instant,
he had disappeared into the liquor store,
     into the bedlam
         of liquid oblivion.

When Nature Questions

The white-tailed deer look at me,
large soulful eyes gazing,
half in sorrow, half in bewilderment.

They seem to question me
about the depletion of their natural habitat,
oh that glorious forest housing nature
within her bosom.

       They seem to question.

*How has it all come down to this,
your disconnection from mother earth?"*

Bloodline for millennium,
habitat housing bodies,
skies nurturing radiant souls.

*How was this slow decline from Eden,
into the hellish inferno
of greed's eternal abyss conceived
then manifested?*

The deer seem to make
a parting statement to me,
before darting off
into the cool evening breeze.

*Change your callous ways of neglect,
before it is too late for your species ...
       as well as ours.*

Room

And into this dream

we are thrown,

just we two, and we shout out

into un-answering heavens, full of stars,

unknowing and winding

in the naivety of infinite hopefulness,

in this room,

in this house love lives

here tonight and always.

Death of Flame Upon a Wood Fire

On closing
the dark chasm
of the past,
her silence,
trembling
velvet lips,
perched as
the raven
hovers above,
held captive,
in dwindled
memory of flame.

Oh that mystery
crackling wildfire
now doused with
tremors of a day
renewed.

Into the Starless Night

The ravage of waves,
brutal and unrelenting,
my flesh and hers lashing out
into starless night,
dashed helpless on jagged rocks
      and undertow.

A revamping of a wandering spirit
weeping for reclusive Eden silence,
the Genius of our re-awakening;
a dream relic, born of ashes,
from the apocalypse.

A wave, vengeful,
her hair tousled and dancing,
her body naked as savage flame.

And here I am wanting nothing more
    than lucid moments
transfixed by the cosmos.

Wilderness

Summer swelter, I remember you,
currently strangling in the present;
now, deer panting, people predicting
our bitter end that is always nigh.

Autumn, you ride your chariot
into our hemisphere; and once again
give birth to your copious kaleidoscope
        of color montage.

        Winter, where are you?

I long to hide, seeking refuge,
        underneath
your frozen lifeless sheets.

Winter, your grandeur
a symphony, composed from
deadening frozen detachment!

Winter, an emotionless wasteland
        of ice
  in which nature hibernates.

Wherein this chilled gloom
my best writing shall emerge
        a caladrius
bursting from the snowy wilderness
        victorious.

We Are Nothing in the Face of Eternity

With the untimely death of you,
transportation darting,
European soul,
set sail at dawn,
and of first light
we sailed yonder.

      I ask of you,
the waves of transcendental youth,
    where have you gone?

Youth stripped us bare and made us old,
a caricature of our former entity,
and yet, this cruel cycle must continue;
we must all go, cradled, entombed,
        nestled within
the naked fiery bosom of earth.

Upon new horizons
intertwined, perplexed;
like a mysterious union of watery grave
and phantoms' stories untold;
still, we unravel, year after year,
upon these ramparts of nothingness;
      a flicker in the cosmos
          of eternity.

Sea Shanty

And as the wind, she changes course,
I am battered lying upon
an unflinching shoreline.

Swirling myth and sweeping tide,
dreams transition,
cast out to angry sea.

Clueless ship, sailing into chaos,
a lone sailor held captive to a dream.

Tombstone requiem intertwined
    with emotionless life,
the beads twirling in stagnant air,
prayers composed, never answered
        with *yes or no.*

While Nature Departs

The leaves of life are toppling,
stark and with the raven's dreams.

A photosynthesis,
drifting upon sunrays;
fathomed, nourished
and soaring.

I feel the tears of a raging sun.
I cannot save this lost and dying world,
         no; not alone.

There is no reason, no promise,
from our leaders poised as snakes.
They embrace folly and fall as clowns;
         and still we follow.

The mountains simmer,
loose in their sockets.
Seasons phase,
switch into yellowed pages
of Armageddon.

     Oceans bake.
Coral reefs surrender
      and die.

Nature follows the corporate
into catastrophe,
shaking us now
into oblivion.

Once in a Lifetime

That chance meeting
with that one person.
Stars collide and two
complex universes
meld into one.

    All sorrows evaporate,
        tears subside,
and the rose tinted glasses
      are always prevalent
through her visions of loveliest hue.

Happiness has healed
the broken hearted.
A touch is a concerto.
Rhapsody of blue veil
has been lifted, exposing light.

A smile revealed,
upon an angel's wings
sunflower petals glistening
in a rain storm that lifted
    when she said ...
        I do.

When it is Time

I sat at the edge of sanity's onslaught
perplexed by this callous world.
Later, insanity encompasses me
like a lunar eclipse.

I do not belong here ...
so I set sail on the morning tide,
galloping amongst waves;
harsh and intrusive,

I shall go, when God calls,
ecstatic upon silken caress
of raven night.

Our Demise

We live in a society
that has become
so afraid of everything,
wrinkles upon flesh,
death in the Winter
      of life.

We live in fear of
boarding planes
and visits to our
local supermarkets.

We live in a society
that's afraid of the final war,
terminus point pending;
exit sign, next horizon.
Armageddon lurking.

We live in a society
that has, on one hand,
become bloated and numb,
while on the other panic driven,
ruled by blinding FEAR and RAGE!

Complacency
has a secret marriage vow,
locked within caldrons
of icy rebuke and cathartic psyche.

Evening Raven Poem

The evening hovers like a curse around me,
     adorned in silken caws of raven,
perched sternly in thick leafed dogwood tree.

There's a Southern oppression
in this Northern town,
fury of tumultuous heat bearing down,
head spinning in an unintelligible smog.

I can hear echoes of my childhood,
fear fully made in the image of God,
in the tiny wood sided Baptist Church
that my mother attended as a child also.

Mr. southern drawl Minister,
fists dropping like lead gavels of fury,
dead upon oak podium of fire and brimstone.

My father was a drinker and a gambling man.
He was born in Washington DC
in the Lutheran faith.
He was an intellectual
and thought his way into atheism
early in life.

Sometimes I believe he comes back
     to visit me,
sometimes in the nightmares of childhood,
    that still haunt me,
 other times in the form of
 a stern and wrathful raven.

Working Hours

Alone, this morning walk,
plank of ice glistening,
alone and hollowed behind
the eyes that are mine.

Soulful, earthy hue,
and doe pants, nibbling from
the shrub's blaze of color.

Stark clouds hovering,
ominous and dead,
like yesterday's visions
thrown and smashed
from heavenly wake.

Red brick fading
as Midwestern dreams collapse,
oblong and spattered,
upon well-manicured lawns.

Ravens caw, squirrels scamper.
   I count the hours
until my shift surrenders
   and I am free again.

As Time Passes

Hammer down, dawn awaits,
    life is fleeting,
and youth has flown away.

Free as a bird my soul will fly,
and what a life and legacy
    left behind.

Feathers fly and dandelions soar.
The night questions, *'why?'*

We have set sail
and conquered our youthful fears.
We have fought earthly wars within.

We have been educated abroad
and come back home,
only to yearn for more adventures;
always the wanderer.

The world we once knew
has become a microcosm,
yet, we yearn for that simplicity
again and again.

Waves

We're part of this game.
Life rolls the dice and we
just roll with the waves.

Waves of hello, and of goodbye.
The pulsating rhythm of waves,
pulling us towards each other,
never parting for long,
dreams and visions,
everything into fruition.

Rivers flow and flowers grow
fading with seasons of stealth;
passing faster still.

Hearts collide, terminus point reached;
always knew that it was you ...
my final destination.

not of this world

this life we are passing through/
lackadaisical/ shouldn't really be/
except for god/ that has allowed/
this being/ I have lived a different
life/ on another planet/ shove this
money driven world/ academic/
implode and descended/ into
depressive woe/ a wound/ the
classic music begins/ and spinning
entwined in fatalism/ i have intellect/
don't care what they say/ laugh behind
my back/ knife in and twist/ wise
beyond all this/ painful life/ cherry
blossoms by the mad house/ the river
cries and sheds our skin/ behind the curtain/
take a bow and leave all this behind/
just leave an epitaph/ of poet/ upon
my stone/ and carry on as though nothing
had ever happened.

Dreams of You

Stars plummet away
from a cosmos that birthed them.
Cumulus clouds, woven,
clutching onto dreams of you
bewildered in jade forest,
never afraid while birds sing.

I feel as I should,
a minute speck of dust,
in your beautiful universe.

    I am nothing
in this vast macrocosm.

    But to you something special.
        I can only hope.

Afterglows

And after forlorn galaxies implode
and the naked bodies in collection
        collide.

And after all rain clouds disperse
and circles have evaporated
in wrecked drunken mind.

The imminent eve of Armageddon
    lays in wait, like a sniper
        seeking asylum
  from the obituary of demise.

Here, woven and interfacing
into kind annellation;
here, looking and longing,
for the calm release
of warm cadence
from Winter oblivion.

And after the waves,
of a wrathful cataclysmic demise
have dragged you down,
into the morning undertow
where oblivion awaits,
it is only then that you will see.

You had this coming to you all along.

Author Profile

Wayne Russell is a poet of Scottish heritage, born and raised in Florida. He later moved to Houston, Texas then Atlanta, Georgia and then full circle back to northern Florida. At the age of eighteen he joined the Army National Guard and a year later, he crossed over into the active Navy. In the early days of Wayne's service, he was stationed to Dunoon, Scotland; from there he continued his travels around the world until his service days ended. Wayne has lived in both Wellington and Palmerston North, in New Zealand. His favorite cities include Edinburgh, Glasgow, Barcelona, Amsterdam, and Brussels.

Wayne has been widely published online and in paperback journals since 2006. His first poem was published via Quill Books in 1989, from there he was hooked; and over the years he has honed his craft and has received a Best of the Net nomination and a Pushcart Prize nomination. His first book, 'Where Angels Fear" was published by Guarilia Genius Press in 2020 and is available on Amazon.

Wayne currently resides in Sout East Ohio with his wife; his soul mate; Jennifer.

Afterword

Firstly, I would like to thank Poet Laureate Emerita of New Westminster, BC, CANADA, Candice James at Silver Bow Publishing, without herx none of this would have been possible. I would like to also thank my children, step children, my intelligent and beautiful wife Jennifer; I would especially like to thank God, for all of this would definitely have not been remotely possible without his kindness and blessing.